VALERIE WESTRA

# Just Add Art

*Home Staging Tips to Make Buyers Fall in Love with Your Home*

Copyright © 2022 by Valerie Westra

All rights reserved. No part of this publication may be reproduced, stored or transmitted in any form or by any means, electronic, mechanical, photocopying, recording, scanning, or otherwise without written permission from the publisher. It is illegal to copy this book, post it to a website, or distribute it by any other means without permission.

Valerie Westra has no responsibility for the persistence or accuracy of URLs for external or third-party Internet Websites referred to in this publication and does not guarantee that any content on such Websites is, or will remain, accurate or appropriate.

First edition

This book was professionally typeset on Reedsy.
Find out more at reedsy.com

# Contents

| | |
|---|---:|
| Introduction | 1 |
| Wall Art | 6 |
| Accessories | 25 |
| Color | 44 |
| Conclusion | 50 |
| References | 52 |
| *About the Author* | 55 |

# Introduction

Welcome to Just Add Art. I'm very excited to write this book for two reasons. First, it's my very first book. And second, I'm passionate about home staging. I never thought that I would write it. I've always thought that I'm not a talented writer. It doesn't come naturally to me. But I decided to challenge myself and here I am.

My name is Valerie Westra and I'm a home stager. From a young age, I was drawn to art and design, but as life happened, my career led me down a different path. It was only after a midlife crisis that resulted in a serious health issue that I took a deep breath, followed my passion, and started a new career. I have loved hanging pictures and rearranging the furniture in my room since I was a teenager, so home staging seemed like the obvious choice. So off I went... It's now been over a decade.

This book is very short, so you can see it's not a complete guide to staging your home. You can find a lot of books with a comprehensive list of things to do to prepare your home for a successful sale. They will include all the steps you need to take: decluttering, cleaning, organizing, depersonalizing, rearranging furniture, etc.

They all are very important steps that lead to the final part of staging known as showcasing. Essentially, it's about decorating your home for someone who will buy it. And this is what this little book is about.

Home staging is marketing. Like any marketing technique, its purpose is to lead the prospect to the sale. Here, to the sale of your home. Indeed, a dirty or cluttered home won't appeal to buyers, but cleanliness is not what will make them fall in love and buy it.

During my home staging career, I've seen many sellers who focus so much on the steps that come before decorating. But they didn't pay attention to or spend any time on what makes their home truly stand out. It's like going on a date after you took a shower and put clean clothes on but forgot to put on makeup and jewelry. Kinda important, isn't it?

I wrote this book with the assumption that you have already taken all the necessary steps mentioned above. Maybe your Realtor told you to do so, or you already knew about home staging. After all, it's been around for a few decades and has become a real estate industry standard in most areas.

Maybe you've read a few books and googled home staging tips. Then you've done cleaning, decluttering, depersonalizing, and even a few very important upgrades. But you feel that something is missing. After your personality leaves your home, there is no excitement and no emotions.

I hope this little book will help you find that missing piece and

## INTRODUCTION

make your home staging project complete. The tips I offer will make your home beautiful and irresistible to buyers. It will create a desire to live in your home happily ever after. And this will lead to a fast and profitable sale.

It's not a complete list of decorating ideas. I don't think it exists. Home staging is a creative process, and just like any creative endeavor, it doesn't have limits. However, it also follows certain tried-and-true rules that bring results.

Art comes in many forms and plays a significant role in enhancing the aesthetic appeal of any space. Most people think of wall art when considering how they can use art in staging and decorating their homes. But let's look at all the various forms of artistic expression that find their place in our homes: accessories, sculptures, textiles, books, light fixtures, etc.

Each art form plays a unique role in creating the desired aesthetic and ambiance within a living space and can transform a mundane space into a warm and welcoming one. From unique plant holders to intricate vases, you can find something for every room in your home.

Sculptures can add a touch of elegance and sophistication to a room, while still being eye-catching and thought-provoking.

Textiles are another art form that adds character and personality while injecting warmth and coziness. From throw pillows to blankets, curtains to area rugs, textiles can inject colors, patterns, and textures into any space. These can complement other pieces of artwork or create a statement on their own.

Books and light fixtures also have decorative value in our homes. Books, in particular, are a functional and stylish way to add a touch of personality and intellectualism to any room. In contrast, light fixtures provide both functional and aesthetic value. Unique and stylish fixtures can create a statement piece in any room while still being functional.

Creating a harmonious combination of diverse forms of art in a home enhances the overall design and creates feelings and emotions that make a house a home and resonate with prospective buyers. When staging or decorating a home, it is essential to consider all the different forms of art available, and how they can contribute to an overall aesthetically pleasing result.

Artists enrich our homes and lives with their talents and visions. They put their heart and soul into bringing these creations to life, and it is our great privilege to showcase their work in the best way possible. Art plays an important role in creating feelings within us when we live in our homes. Now, it's time to create those same feelings for buyers and help them fall in love with our homes, too.

Since the beginning of time, people have been drawn to creating and enjoying art. Looking at art can make us laugh, cry, or sometimes cringe. It creates memories and associations. It can make rooms look larger, and ceilings higher. It makes focal points stand out. It enhances the style of the house. Most importantly, it creates the desire in buyers to live in this home, to live the lifestyle you portrayed, and to be a part of the picture you painted for them. And they start feeling what you want them to feel.

**_Feeling at home._**

# Wall Art

Many times I met home sellers who decluttered their homes to the extreme. They tell me they packed everything up, including the pictures they had on the walls, in order not to distract the buyers from the features of the property. But wall art can emphasize and enhance the home's features. It can lead the eye to what's most important in every room. Everyone knows about focal points, and wall art is one of the best ways to highlight them.

There are a few different types of wall art, and not all of them work well for home staging. Let's look at those that do.

Original Art

When selecting art for staging, it's essential to pay attention to the difference between original art and reproductions.

Original art refers to a one-of-a-kind piece created by an artist. It could be a painting, a sculpture, or a photograph, and it carries a unique personality and character that cannot be replicated.

Reproductions, on the other hand, are prints or copies of an original artwork created to mimic the look of the original piece. While they may appear similar to the original, they lack the authenticity and uniqueness of the original artwork.

Original art is the most effective type of art to use in home staging, in my opinion.

Why do we pay a hundredfold for originals vs reproductions? It's not just because the artist created it and it is unique. It looks and feels different; it emanates different energy and radiates a different vibe. Can you feel it when you are in a gallery standing close to a painting? The energy is sometimes subtle, sometimes palpable, almost tangible. If you have this type of art in your home, the buyers will feel it too. So it's important to choose paintings that create a positive vibe. Some paintings can be quite disturbing.

Why else is original art essential in home staging? Another reason is that it adds character to a space. When you use original art for staging, you achieve a personalized and sophisticated look, a unique touch, and a more elevated and luxurious feel. It sets your property apart from other similar properties in the same market.

Original art elevates a property's perceived value by communicating a sense of exclusivity. It has a way of evoking emotions and creating personal connections with buyers and they can envision themselves living in this space. Therefore, it increases their likelihood of making an offer.

Investing in original art is always worthwhile, and there are plenty of avenues to discover and purchase unique pieces. Art galleries, auctions, and contemporary art fairs are excellent places to explore different styles and mediums to find what suits the property and your budget. Supporting local artists is another great way to acquire original artwork while adding a personal touch when staging your home.

Choosing original art over reproductions is essential in creating beautiful, personalized, and sophisticated homes to maximize the potential of a property. Investing in original art is always worthwhile and can make all the difference in a successful home staging project.

But, of course, original paintings can be expensive, and perhaps you didn't plan to spend this kind of money. Your next best bet is to rent them (from a local gallery, or directly from the artists) or buy reproductions.

## Reproductions

While reproductions may seem like a cost-effective alternative, there are several drawbacks to consider. Low-quality reproductions lack depth and texture, leaving a room feeling dull and standardized. A home staging project that uses reproductions can fall flat, failing to inspire potential buyers or tenants. Therefore, it's important to use high-quality reproductions like giclee.

Giclee prints have become a popular choice for reproductions of original paintings in home staging because of their high quality and ability to be printed on various surfaces. Giclee prints are created using inkjet technology, which provides high accuracy, color vibrancy, and depth that closely resemble the original artwork. As a result, giclee prints are often preferred over other forms of reproductions, such as lithographs or offset prints.

One advantage of giclee prints is that they can be printed on a variety of surfaces, including paper, canvas, and even metal. This provides home stagers with endless options to bring visual charm to a property, whether it be large canvases for a living room or smaller prints for bedrooms and hallways. The versatility of giclee prints means they can be tailored to match any interior design style, from traditional to modern and everything in between.

Another benefit of giclee prints is their cost-effectiveness. Original paintings can be expensive and out of reach for many homeowners, while giclee prints provide a more affordable alternative. This makes it easier to invest in art for a property, which can ultimately increase its value and appeal.

Besides giclee prints, there are other forms of reproductions that can be used as art in home staging. Lithographs are created using a printing process that involves plates with images etched onto them, which are then pressed onto paper to create a print. While lithographs are also high-quality reproductions, they may lack the depth and color vibrancy of giclee prints. Offset prints are mass-produced prints that have a lower quality compared to other forms of reproductions.

## Photography

Artistic photography that is, and not photos of your wedding or your kids. You probably know that those don't have a place in your home when it's on the market. If you aren't sure, here is why: people are drawn to personal photos during showings. "Oh, such cute kids!"; "Where did they have their wedding? Is this Hawaii?" Comments like these show that the buyers are distracted from touring your house and they interrupt the flow. They already know it's someone else's house, and now they even know who the owners are. This makes it much more difficult for them to feel at home. Personal photographs can distract potential buyers, as they may not envision themselves living in a space that is filled with photos of someone's family and life. In addition, personal photographs can limit a buyer's appeal by making the home feel too specific to the seller's taste and preferences.

On the other hand, beautiful artistic photographs can add depth and character to a staged home, creating a unique and visually interesting environment that can attract potential buyers.

Artistic photographs can complement a variety of decor styles, from modern and minimalist to traditional and rustic. For example, a black-and-white photograph of a city skyline can give a modern space a sophisticated and sleek feel, while a colorful landscape can complement a more traditional style. In addition, photographs of interesting objects or textures, such as a vintage camera or a rusted metal door, can add a touch of character and personality to a staged home.

When selecting and displaying artistic photographs, it is important to ensure that they enhance the overall staging experience. Select photos based on their visual appeal, as well as their ability to complement the decor style of the home. They should be displayed with attention paid to their size, placement, and framing.

Landscapes, still-lives, and cityscapes are the best for home staging, both in color and black and white.

Three-dimensional Art.

3D wall art stands out for its ability to create a sculpture-like effect that can add depth and texture to any room. Using wood, metal, fabric, macramé, or mixed media in creating 3D wall art allows for endless possibilities in design and style. It is an effective way to add interest to a room and create an appealing focal point. However, while 3D wall art can significantly enhance the ambiance of a space, it is crucial to be mindful of its impact.

As a rule of thumb, avoid overpowering pieces that may draw undue attention and distract buyers from the overall look and feel of the house. The goal of 3D wall art in home staging is to complement the room, not to dominate it. Therefore, it is best to select pieces that blend well with the décor and color scheme of the room and enhance its visual appeal.

Whether you're staging a living room, bedroom, or even a bathroom, 3D wall art can be used effectively. For instance, metal artwork can create a stylish and trendy focal point in a home office. A macramé or textile art can be used in a living room to create a cozy and relaxed ambiance. The use of 3D art in home staging is not limited to the walls. Sculptures on tabletops and other surfaces will add visual interest. This form of art will be covered in the next chapter.

Using 3D wall art in home staging can add a touch of sophistication and elegance to the overall look and feel of the property. However, to enhance its effectiveness and prevent it from becoming an overwhelming distraction, it is essential to select tasteful pieces that complement the décor of the room. By doing so, you create a well-balanced ambiance that appeals to potential buyers.

## Posters

One decor item that can sometimes be overlooked and sometimes overused in the home staging process is posters. While posters can add personality and character to a space, it's important to use them strategically.

It's important to consider the type of room in which you are considering adding posters. Rooms that are associated with posters include a teenager's bedroom, a home theater room, or a bar. These are spaces where the posters will add to the overall ambiance of the room and can help to create a specific atmosphere that will appeal to potential buyers.

However, it's also important to keep in mind that in some homes, posters may be completely out of place. For example, if you're staging a luxury home, posters may not fit the overall aesthetic and make the property look cheap. It might turn off potential buyers. In these instances, it's best to rely on original paintings to create a cohesive and sophisticated look.

If you decide to incorporate posters into your staging, it's important to remember not to overuse them. Whether you're using them in a themed room or simply including them as an accent piece, it's important to strike a balance between having enough to make an impact without overwhelming the space. Consider using just one or two posters in a room and make sure they complement the other decor elements.

Ultimately, posters can play a role in home staging, but it's important to use them thoughtfully. Consider the space, the overall aesthetic, and how they will be received by potential buyers. With these factors in mind, you can use posters to add a touch of personality to a room without jeopardizing the overall look and feel of your home.

## Mirrors

Mirrors are the miracle workers of home staging and a staple accessory in every home. Apart from being functional, mirrors can transform and enhance the aesthetics of any space. Depending on the frame and shape, mirrors can work as art pieces easily. Apart from their decorative purpose, mirrors have a more practical use, which is to enhance the lighting and space of any room.

One of the most important aspects of home staging is creating a bright and spacious atmosphere. Mirrors are a key tool in achieving this ambiance. Hanging a mirror in a dark room across a window can reflect the natural light and make the room brighter. This technique not only illuminates the space but also creates an illusion of an enlarged room, making it appear bigger than it actually is. By hanging a mirror to reflect the ocean or a green space view from the window, you can bring the outside in and have a landscape on your wall.

When hanging mirrors, it is essential to consider the placement. While they can expand and brighten spaces, it's important not to hang them where they reflect nothing or something unattractive. For instance, one popular place to hang mirrors is over the fireplace. However, it is only suitable if the fireplace is across the window with a beautiful view. Otherwise, they may reflect the ceiling, becoming useless and a waste of space.

Another strategic placement for mirrors is by the front door. Not only do they have the practical use of having a last-minute check of hair and makeup before heading out, but they also allow buyers to catch their reflection before leaving. However, according to Feng Shui principles, one should not see their reflection as soon as they enter the home, as it creates a negative energy pull. On the other hand, seeing their reflection before leaving the house can give buyers a sense of closure and a feeling of leaving their own home.

Mirrors have the power to enhance the aesthetics of any room, expand the space, and create a bright and spacious atmosphere. When used correctly, mirrors can transform any space and elevate its aura. So, the next time you are planning to stage your home, remember to incorporate mirrors to achieve a magical transformation.

## Wall Art to Avoid in Home Staging

### Gallery walls

I love gallery walls, and I have a few in my house.

In interior design, gallery walls are a popular trend that has taken the world by storm. With their eclectic mix of art and photography arranged in creative layouts, gallery walls can add a touch of personality and style to any space. However, while they may be a beloved feature in your own home, it is important to consider their impact when selling your property.

Gallery walls are typically quite large, covering entire walls and often comprising multiple frames and pieces of art. While they can be a striking addition to a room, they also have the potential to be overwhelming and distracting. When potential buyers are viewing your home, you want them to appreciate all of its features, which can be difficult when a gallery wall takes over the room.

If you have a gallery wall in your house, I suggest removing or replacing it with a single piece of art. This will allow buyers to more easily envision their own style in the space, and prevent your gallery wall from overshadowing other features of the room.

The key to selling your home is to create a space that is appealing to a wide range of buyers. While gallery walls (especially those with family photos) may be a beloved feature in your own home, they will not be the best choice for showcasing your property.

*Signs*

Signs have become a popular trend in interior design as well. We consider them as a way of personalizing one's living space and adding a touch of uniqueness to it. However, it is important to be mindful of the number of signs being used within a space, as they can become overwhelming and even tacky.

Using signs for staging your home can be unappealing and end up projecting poor taste. It's not uncommon to come across homes where every wall is adorned with signs that have religious or "cute" quotes, which I do not recommend using at all. You need to be mindful of the quality of signs and the messages they carry if you decide to use them.

If you have a farmhouse-style home or an industrial-style condo, you can still incorporate signs into the space, as long as they are of high quality. For instance, a large rustic wooden sign with a bold font that carries a simple message can be enough to add style and personalization to a farmhouse kitchen. Industrial-style condos may benefit from using signs with bold typography and a minimalist feel to create an edgy feeling.

It's important to remember that signs should complement the overall feel of your home and not take away from it. If you're unsure about how to incorporate signs in your living space, it's better to play it safe and avoid them altogether.

Signs can be great for adding personality to your living spaces. But because they are very personal, very specific to one's taste, and often are not the best quality, they can be annoying to buyers. I do not recommend them for home staging.

## Decals and Murals

Not a good idea. While they may seem like a fun and creative way to add personality to a space, they can detract from the overall appeal. People may think that the wall is damaged under the decals or that it will be very difficult to remove a mural. I recommend removing any decals that you already have in your home and painting over the murals with the same paint color as the rest of the room. The only exception to this rule may be if you have them in a nursery or kids' room and your kids just can't say goodbye to them. Even then, it's important to keep these decorations to a minimum. In home staging, less is more.

## Styles and Subjects of Wall Art

Not all styles and subjects of wall art will work to stage a home. To ensure that your home is staged properly, it is important to know which styles and themes of wall art will work best for each room. The best styles overall are abstract, florals, landscape, cityscape, still life, vintage, and spa.

As I mentioned earlier, the first thing to consider is the emotions that you want to evoke in each room. When staging a bedroom, you want to create a sense of relaxation and calmness. For this reason, it is best to use artwork that features an ocean or mountain view. By doing so, you can convey a sense of serenity and tranquility to potential buyers. A large painting over the bed can also serve as a headboard if you don't have one and will emphasize the bed as the focal point of the room.

In the ensuite bathroom, it is essential to create a spa-like atmosphere. The best way to achieve this is by using "spa art," which usually features a zen theme with rocks, candles, small fountains, waterfalls, orchids, and other natural elements. These pieces will help create a sanctuary where potential buyers can visualize themselves relaxing after a long day.

Maps are perfect for a home office, a study, or a kid's room. They provide a sense of adventure and exploration, making them an excellent choice for rooms that inspire curiosity and creativity.

For staging a dining room, still lives works incredibly well. This type of art features tranquil scenes of objects such as fruits, flowers, and household objects. These pieces will bring a sense of being grounded and balanced in your space, creating a hospitable atmosphere for potential buyers.

You can use landscape and cityscape art in the living room. These themes provide a sense of openness and unity with the surrounding environment, making them excellent choices for simulating family time, socializing, and relaxation.

For staging a nursery, it is best to use artwork that portrays or features animals in illustrations, such as books or mystical creatures, which create an imaginative world that stimulates the mind and sparks curiosity.

Even though I recommend matching the art style with the style of the house (traditional, farmhouse, coastal, contemporary, industrial, etc.) it's safe to say that abstract art can be used in any style of home. It is a versatile style that can create interest and add a whimsical touch to a room. While traditional homes might feel eclectic when abstract art is used, it will still be effective in creating a unique space that stands out in the minds of potential buyers.

I do not recommend the following styles for staging: portraits of any kind, nudes, political art, and religious art. Use images of animals carefully because wildlife animals can look aggressive and create uneasy feelings.

It is essential to choose pieces that create positive emotions and evoke the feelings that you want to portray in each room. To achieve harmony, try your best to use pictures of the same style or those that have common elements. For example, similar frames or a consistent color scheme.

## Best Wall Art Sizes

Wall art is here to make an impact and it can make or break a room's aesthetic. And choosing the right art size can be a daunting task. It can make the room look cramped and cluttered if the art is too small, and it can be overwhelming if it's too big.

I recommend using larger format art 99% of the time as a standard rule. Among the best sizes to choose from are 48X36, 48X48, and 48X60. These sizes are perfect for most walls, as they can create a significant impact on the room's ambiance. However, it is crucial to note that a large painting can be overpowering if it hangs too close to the entry and takes up the entire wall. Therefore, there should be enough distance for viewers to see the painting without having to move their heads, and enough wall space around it.

Small paintings can cause visual clutter, chopping up the walls. The smallest sizes recommended would be 36X36 or 30X40. If you choose a size smaller than this, it would be best to hang them in bathrooms, put them on open shelves in the kitchen, or serve as decor items in bookcases. Additionally, grouping two smaller paintings can create the illusion of one large painting. But, I do not recommend grouping over two pieces, as this may look too cluttered.

It is crucial to match the size and orientation of the wall to the size and orientation of the picture. This means that you should not hang a landscape-orientation picture on a portrait-orientation wall, and vice versa. Doing so will create a sense of imbalance that will not do your room any good.

Finally, it is vital to note that the picture's width should not exceed the furniture piece it hangs over. The ideal size is the same width as the couch, console table, or headboard, or about 75% of its width. Alternatively, it can be the same size as the opening of the fireplace.

The best wall art sizes are those that create a significant impact on the room's ambiance. Remember that it is vital to keep in mind the size of the room, the distance of the viewer from the painting, and the size of the furniture it hangs over. Following these guidelines ensures your wall art enhances the aesthetic value of your room.

## How and Where to Hang Art

Art hanging is an important aspect of interior decoration. Proper placement of art not only enhances the beauty of the room but also creates a welcoming environment. Professional art hanging is a mix of art and science, and it is a specialized skill that requires experience and knowledge. It should be a topic for a separate book. While we are not striving to be professionals, following a few simple rules can help create a cohesive environment and balance with other elements of your decor.

## Placement of Art

For some unknown reason, one of the most common mistakes people make while hanging artwork is placing it too high. It can make it uncomfortable to view the art, causing neck strain. The center of the picture should be at or around 57 inches from the floor, which is considered the average eye level and is used in art galleries. If you hang art over a mantel or a couch, it should be 6 to 8 inches above them.

Following these rules, your art will be balanced and create a feeling of harmony. Use a level to make sure the picture is 100% horizontal as it conveys professionalism and attention to detail. There is nothing worse than a crooked picture! We have a built-in level inside us based on the fact that the horizon is always horizontal. Anything that looks "off" may create profound discomfort in your buyers.

Avoid hanging artwork on narrow walls, such as between doors and windows, on either side of windows, and in narrow hallways. It can cause the room to look choppy, and it will be difficult for buyers to keep their attention on the important features of the room. Hanging a picture at the end of the hallway will bring it visually closer and draw the eye toward it.

## Emphasizing Focal Points

When it comes to staging a room, choosing a focal point is essential. It creates a point of interest and sets the tone for the entire space. Focal points can be anything from a beautiful fireplace to a stunning view outside.

Pictures are an excellent asset to emphasize focal points over the mantel, a bed, and a couch in the conversation area. Hanging a large, stylized art over the desk in an office can create a powerful statement.

In some cases, the focal point may be a window. Windows are an excellent natural source of light, and they often offer stunning views. In such cases, choosing to hang artwork beside the window may not be the best option. Instead, the window can play the role of a picture, and no additional artwork is required. Doing so ensures that the view is the focus of the room.

## *Symmetry Creates Harmony*

Symmetry creates a balanced and harmonious feeling in a room. If it's not possible to hang a picture over the mantel or over the headboard, hanging two similar-sized pictures on both sides creates visual symmetry and is pleasing to look at. If it's not possible to hang pictures symmetrically on both sides, balance can be achieved by placing a tall accessory, a floor lamp, or a floor plant on the other side.

Art hanging is an important aspect of interior decoration and home staging. It requires balance and harmony to create a welcoming environment. By following the guidelines mentioned above, you can create an environment that is balanced with other elements of your decor. Proper placement of art leads to a visually appealing room and creates a feeling of comfort and harmony, which is your home staging goal.

# Accessories

Let's talk about another form of art: accessories. They are a wonderful decorating tool that adds visual interest, ties different parts of the room together, adds color and spark, and helps lead the eye to the important features of the room. There is an unlimited amount of different accessories you can use to bring life to the rooms.

Just like with wall art, accessories should be of a large or medium size. You should avoid using small decor items alone, but you can group them with larger ones to create a vignette.

The number of accessories used in one room depends on the size of the room and the number of pieces of furniture in the room. This is where the principle "less is more" plays an important role. To err on the safe side, remove 10% of accessories after you place them. I know you tried hard to make the room look good, but seriously, just do it. It's much less noticeable when there is a "lack" of accessories than when there are too many. It's so easy to create visual clutter or to ruin balance by adding just one more item. An excellent exercise is to leave the room for a few minutes, do something unrelated, then come back and follow your gut feeling. You may have to do it a few times before you get it right. And then it hits you: yes, that's it!

Placing accessories the right way comes with practice, like any skill.

It's worth investing a bit of money in accessories for staging because you can also use them in your new home. Believe me, you'll have so much fun choosing and placing them, you'll want to keep them.

With such an enormous number of different accessories in stores and online, which ones do you choose? There are a few staging-friendly ones that work well in any space.

## Books

Books have always been a significant source of inspiration, entertainment, and knowledge. You may not be thinking of books as decorative accessories, but they absolutely are, and I love decorating with books. Depending on the books' styles, they can create a feeling of sophistication or fun, an aura of history or romance, and most definitely add color. If you're looking to add some personality and character to your living space, there are many ways to incorporate books into your home decor.

One of the easiest ways to use books as decorative accessories is by stacking them. Stacking books can create a chic stylish look, especially if the books are of different sizes and have unique covers. You can place them on a coffee table, bookshelf, or even on the floor to add visual interest and height to a vignette. Stacks of books can also be used to adjust the height of decor items in an arrangement to make it look harmonious and balanced.

Books can also create an intriguing centerpiece or focal point. A pile of books topped with a vase of flowers creates a beautiful arrangement that captures the attention of anyone who enters the room. You can also place books under a glass coffee table to add a literary touch to your living space.

Think of an open book on a comfy chair by the window... you just want to enjoy a quiet moment in this reading nook! A colorful cookbook on the kitchen counter will help buyers imagine cooking delicious meals for family and friends.

Another way to incorporate books into your home decor is by using them as a backdrop for other decorative items. Books can serve as a perfect prop for picture frames, vases, sculptures, or any other decorative item that you want to showcase. You can also use them as a platform for a lamp or any other statement piece that you want to highlight.

Choosing the right books for your decor can make a big difference in the overall ambiance of the space. For example, leather-bound books, vintage books, and hardcovers with glossy covers can add a sense of class and sophistication to any room. Art books, decor magazines, and encyclopedias make a chic way to add a pop of color. You can add any books with bright covers to your space. However, avoid paperbacks.

Incorporating books into your home's decor is not only classy and timeless but also eco-friendly and budget-friendly. You can find good books for staging your home at secondhand stores, garage sales, or even in your home library. With a little creativity and imagination, the possibilities are endless.

## How to style bookshelves

Styling bookshelves has become an art form, and with the rise of social media, everyone wants their bookshelves to be Pinterest or Instagram-worthy. However, many people have books crammed on bookshelves in a mismatched manner, mixed up in various sizes, colors, and styles. Now is the time to fix it and put your books to work.

There are different ways to decorate bookshelves. You can color block them, collecting books of similar colors together so that each shelf has a different hue. I decorated one of my bookcases this way. It takes a bit of time to do it, especially if you have a lot of books, but if you don't, then you can still do the color block style with the addition of other decor items. Which is the best way to decorate, anyway.

You can combine books with decorative items like candles, framed pictures, vases and sculptures, glass and ceramics, etc. Well, pretty much anything! Take inspiration from nature and use greenery or flowers to add color and freshness to your bookshelf. Small potted plants, fresh flowers, or artificial greenery can give your bookshelf a vibrant look.

ACCESSORIES

You can use your mementos, but remember, nothing personal. Nothing with names, and no personal photos. However, artistic photos work well, as I mentioned in the previous chapter.

Again, it's important not to create visual clutter. Leave the shelves ⅓ empty. If your house is traditional, you can have more books on the shelves, but for a modern look, opt for half-empty shelves.

What decor items to use also depends on the color of your bookcases: white with the white back panel, or dark. Make sure the objects you use don't blend in with the background.

When placing the books and decor items on the shelves, alternate smaller and larger items, horizontal and vertical stacks of books, and colorful and neutral objects. If you have a distinctive color scheme in the room that comes from wall art, furniture, or accessories, then make sure you use this color on the shelves as well.

Don't strive to do a symmetrical arrangement. It will be difficult to do and it will look very static. Asymmetry is best for the shelves.

Just like decorating other places, step outside for a few minutes, do something different, and then come back. Chances are, one or two things will jump out at you as not balanced or looking "off". Play with it and eventually, you'll get it right.

It's not just bookcases in your living room or office. Open kitchen shelves will look spectacular if you style them, and might become a focal point of your kitchen.

Use colorful cookbooks and pretty kitchenware as the bookends. Potted herbs look lovely not just on windowsills but on the shelves as well. This is one place where you can place a sign with a food-related quote.

Another place to style shelves is in the laundry room. Your laundry room may be boring, but it doesn't have to be. Perhaps don't place books, but put your laundry supplies in pretty containers, add small pots with silk greenery, and lean a couple of framed pictures. Your laundry room just got a facelift and buyers will like that. After all, we are showing them how their life can be in this home, and that even doing laundry can be an aesthetically pleasing experience!

Well, this turned out to be a longer section of my book than I expected. You can tell that I love styling shelves! I could write more and more, but I included a link with shelf styling ideas in the resources section.

Textiles

Textiles play a crucial role in completing the look and feel of any room. They provide the perfect finishing touch, adding warmth, texture, and color to your home décor. From mid-century modern to bohemian chic, textiles can help you create any style you desire. The right use of textiles has the power to transform a plain room into a cozy retreat or a luxurious haven.

## ACCESSORIES

Whether you're staging your house for sale, designing a new room, or updating your existing one, textiles are a must-have. Incorporating them into your design will help create depth and interest, providing the perfect opportunity to add character and personality. Soft furnishings such as rugs, throws, curtains, and accent cushions can add warmth to your interiors, while visual accents such as baskets, tapestries, and macramé add texture and visual interest.

Tapestries and macramé add a bohemian vibe to your interiors. Use them as wall décor, headboards, or even as room dividers. They add a cozy and textured feel to your interiors while also providing a visual accent.

Curtains are another essential textile in any room. They provide privacy and block sunlight while also adding a decorative accent to the room. Curtains come in various patterns and colors, allowing you to get creative and choose a style that works.

### Rugs

In home staging, the little things can make all the difference. One important item to consider is the usage of rugs. Rugs add warmth, color, and depth to a room, but it's important to follow a few rules to use them correctly and effectively.

The two best sizes for rugs to use in home staging are 5X7 and 8X10. These sizes are versatile and work in various rooms and spaces. Rugs are used to define the areas of open-concept rooms, whether it be a dining area or a conversation area. Defining these spaces can help buyers envision themselves living and using the space more effectively.

When using a rug under a dining table, it's important to make sure that all chairs' legs are on the rug. This helps ensure a cohesive and visually appealing look, and it also prevents accidents such as chairs slipping on the floor. In the living or family room, the front legs of the couch and armchairs should be on the rug as well. This helps to visually anchor the furniture in the space.

While rugs can add visual interest to a room, it's important to make sure that any beautiful hardwood floors are not completely covered. The floors are an important feature of a home and potential buyers will want to see them.

Another important rule to follow when using rugs is to never use them on carpeted floors. It looks cluttered and detracts from the overall aesthetic of the room.

When choosing a rug, it's important to avoid large and bright patterns. A little of an accent color is nice to have, but the rug shouldn't be overpowering and take all the attention away from other features of the room. It's best to choose a color that is repeated in other elements of the room, which helps create a cohesive look and flow.

It's best to use faux animal hides when incorporating rugs into your staging design. By using these types of rugs, you respect buyers who may be vegetarians, vegans, animal lovers, and animal rights activists – all of whom are a significant segment of the population and deserve to be taken into consideration.

By following a few simple rules, rugs will add warmth, color, and depth to a room and help buyers envision themselves living and using the space.

## Accent cushions and throws

Accent cushions and throws are essential decorative items that can transform the look and feel of any room in your home. These versatile accessories come in various sizes, shapes, fabrics, and colors, making it easy to mix and match to create a stylish look.

One of the best ways to use accent cushions and throws is on a couch or an armchair. Not only do they add a pop of color, but they also provide an extra layer to create feelings of comfort and coziness. You can use different shapes and sizes of cushions to create a layered effect. For example, mix and match square and rectangular cushions for a modern look or use large oversized cushions for a more relaxed feel.

Throws are perfect for draping over a couch or an armchair, adding texture, dimension, and warmth to the room. They come in a variety of materials such as wool, cotton, and cashmere, so you can choose the one that suits the style of the room.

If you have a bench in your foyer, adding cushions and throws can create a cozy and welcoming vignette. A wicker basket filled with throws is perfect for storing them while also adding a decorative touch to the room. Sometimes I put a throw on an office chair. Combined with a rug, it makes the home office so much more cozy.

You can also use cushions and throws in the bedrooms to create an inviting setting. Adding a throw at the foot of the bed creates a layered effect, while a pile of cushions adds height and extra dimension to the room.

Transform a twin bed in a spare bedroom into a daybed by moving its long side to the wall and adding a bunch of cushions. Hang a picture over the bed and you have a beautiful focal point.

In the principal bedroom, there is no better way to create a peaceful retreat or a luxurious romantic feeling than with textiles. Crisp white linens, a hotel-style quilt, and down-filled accent pillows will elevate the bed to its full potential and will impress the buyers. This is the bedroom they've always dreamed of! Honestly, in my over a decade of work as a home stager, I haven't seen tons of luxurious hotel-style bedrooms. Everyone wants to have one, but not too many homeowners take the time to create it. When the buyers see the bedroom they want, your home will inspire them as nothing else will. So go ahead, and invest in new linens, bedding, and cushions. You will not only impress the buyers but treat yourself - you deserve it and now is the time.

For a more intense touch feeling, use different fabrics of cushions and throws. Depending on the style of each room, you can use cotton, silk, denim, knits, wool, linen, etc. You can combine solid and patterns for more interest. Make sure that the colors work with your overall color scheme.

Don't use your cushions if they're old and flat. Invest in new ones that are full and fluffy.

There are tons of ways to style with accent cushions, so I included a link with some of them for you in the reference section.

## Baskets

Baskets are not just functional storage pieces, they add a unique touch to any room of the house. They come in various shapes, sizes, and materials such as seagrass, bamboo, willow, and vines. These natural materials create a sculpture-like look and provide a fantastic tactile sensation. You can use them in any room, including the bedrooms, the living room, and the laundry room.

In the bedroom, fill baskets with fluffy throws or extra pillows, adding both texture and warmth to the room. Baskets can store vintage books or as a catch-all for remote controls and other miscellaneous items in the living room. In the laundry room, baskets can organize laundry supplies, such as detergent, fabric softener, and dryer sheets.

Baskets can also serve as an alternative to planters and are useful for floor plants. The natural material of the baskets creates a lovely contrast to the greenery of the plants, adding to the natural ambiance of the space.

Another area where baskets come in handy is closets, cabinets, and cupboards. When potential buyers are viewing a house, they open doors to closets and cabinets to see how spacious the storage is. To create a stylish and organized appearance, pack away seasonal clothes and store them in an outside storage area. Then, use attractive baskets to hold any "messy" items such as shoes, bags, or toiletries.

By using baskets to organize and decorate a space, potential buyers will be excited about the beautifully organized lifestyle they always wanted and that can be achieved in the house. With a little creativity and a few baskets, you can transform any room into a stylish and organized haven.

## Curtains

One of the crucial elements of home decorating is choosing the right window treatments. Although curtains can enhance the room's ambiance and appearance, I do not always suggest their use in home staging.

Curtains can make a room look smaller and darker. Having curtains that are too heavy or dark can make a room feel cramped and uninviting, which can turn off buyers. Curtains can distract and take attention away from the room's features. If the curtains are too bold or have an eye-catching pattern, they can divert the buyer's attention away from the room's focal point.

However, having no curtains at all can make a room feel too

bare.

To avoid these negative effects, I recommend light-colored, sheer curtains that allow natural light to filter through the windows.

If you don't have curtains already, they can be costly and time-consuming to install. Home staging is all about making the most of the existing features of a house, and adding custom curtains can be an unnecessary expense. By avoiding curtains, or using simple rods and inexpensive sheer curtains, you can save time and money and focus on enhancing other areas of the home.

There are a few situations when you do want to use high-quality curtains.

One of the key benefits of curtains is their ability to minimize the look of unattractive windows. If you have outdated, mismatched, or small windows, curtains can help to draw attention away from these imperfections. Simply by hanging a set of elegant and more substantial curtains, you can give the room an instant upgrade. This is particularly important when trying to appeal to potential buyers who may scrutinize every detail of a property.

Another key reason to use curtains in home staging is for privacy. If your home is located close to a main road or a busy footpath, curtains can help to block out prying eyes. This is especially important in homes with ground-floor bedrooms or living areas. By adding a layer of privacy, homeowners can create a sense of comfort and security that can be appealing to buyers.

Finally, curtains are essential in bedrooms where they add a touch of comfort and block the light for a night of better sleep. In a primary bedroom, for example, sheer curtains can create a romantic and relaxing ambiance. Meanwhile, blackout curtains can block out light and noise, creating a peaceful space for restful sleep. This is important in areas with early morning sun or noise from outside.

Tapestries and Macramé

Two popular decorative techniques used in home staging are tapestry and macramé.

Tapestry is a centuries-old decorative technique that involves weaving different fibers together to create intricate, colorful designs. It has become a popular choice for home staging as it adds a touch of culture and sophistication to a room. A tapestry can create a focal point that draws the eye. You can also drape it over a sofa, chair, or bed to add color and texture to a space. Tapestry comes in a variety of patterns, shapes, and sizes, ranging from bold and bright to muted and understated.

Macramé involves knotting together threads or cords to create patterns and designs. It has a more bohemian or ethnic feel and is ideal for adding warmth and creativity to a room. Macramé can be used in a variety of ways in home decor, from wall hangings to plant hangers to curtains. However, in home staging, limit the use of macrame as wall hangings only to add interest and texture to a blank wall and if you have macrame plant hangers, remove them because they create a cluttered look.

When using tapestry or macrame in home staging, it is important to keep a few things in mind. First, less is more. Use these decorative techniques sparingly to add interest without overwhelming a space. Second, it is important to choose pieces that fit the overall design style of the space, are high quality, and don't look tacky.

## Plants

There is no better way - literally and figuratively - to bring life to a space than with plants. Home stagers call plants "a secret weapon". Everyone loves plants. Even people with a brown thumb often continue buying them, hoping one day they develop a green thumb. That's why dressing up your home with plants will appeal to any and every buyer. Plants are a magical element in decor, adding a touch of nature's beauty to any space. Not only do plants clean the air, but they can also fill empty spaces, add layers of colors and textures, and create a focal point that draws the eye. Plants fit perfectly in any style of decor and can be used in every room to elevate the visual appeal of your space.

Adding a touch of nature outside your home sets the tone for the rest of the decor. Two urns overflowing with flowers at the front door create an inviting entrance, while a vase or planter full of flowers in the foyer can jazz up the welcome vibe. Potted plants can work perfectly indoors too. A large bouquet of fresh flowers or a professionally done flower arrangement on the dining table will not only create a focal point but also enhance the ambiance of the dining room.

Plants can add depth and interest to any room. They can make a small bedroom feel more romantic with the simple addition of a small vase filled with mini-roses. If you have a window with a view of the garden, place a plant in front of it to bring the garden view inside and transform the room into an extension of the garden. A white orchid in the bathroom brings the luxurious feeling of a high-end spa.

Add a plant to your desk to make the home office feel more cozy. Potted succulents work perfectly as decor items on open shelves, and potted herbs on the kitchen windowsill create an attractive mini-garden.

Adding plants to all rooms in your home can give a cohesive and natural feel. Small plants in cute planters can adorn side tables, nightstands, and console tables to accentuate your decor. But, remember, less is more. It's vital not to overdo it by putting too many plants on the same surface or in the same room.

Remember, healthy plants generate positive energy, but dry, neglected, dusty, or dying plants generate negative energy. I do not recommend cacti plants for staging because of their symbolic negativity in certain rooms. So for a safe measure, it's better to avoid them.

I mentioned people with a brown thumb. If you are one of them, don't despair. If you don't have a green thumb or the time to maintain plants, good-quality artificial plants will work the same way. Just ensure they look realistic and that you care for them, as they show dust easily. I included a link to good-quality artificial plants in the resources section.

Plants add freshness and life to any decor style. By making a conscious choice to add some greenery, you can create cohesive and attractive decor that breathes life into your space.

## Biophilic Design

This book won't be complete without a word about biophilic design. Even before COVID, it was estimated that ⅔ of the Earth's population lived in urban areas and spent 90% of their time indoors. The pandemic forced us to look at how we live in our homes. Most of us now want our homes to be a sanctuary and a place to recharge, unwind, and unplug - and not a place to store stuff. When home buyers look for their new home or their first home, this is what they want this home to be. This is where biophilic design helps.

Biophilic design is an innovative design approach that emphasizes the connection between nature and human beings. It incorporates elements of nature into indoor spaces to create a more welcoming and comfortable environment. Biophilic design has been gaining popularity lately, with people increasingly seeking a connection with nature in their daily lives.

It doesn't mean that you have to redesign your home before you sell it. When staging your home, you can apply a few biophilic design principles of connecting people and nature and generating energy for well-being and good quality of life. These principles will address the air quality in your home and create more harmony, balance, and a seamless transition between indoors and outdoors.

Some of the essential biophilic design elements include color, water, sunlight, plants, natural materials, beautiful views, and fire. For instance, including plenty of plants in the interior space is one of the easiest ways to add some biophilic design elements. Plants have a positive impact on mood and health, and they can improve air quality by removing harmful toxins from the air.

Sunlight is another important element of biophilic design because it can have a major impact on mental and physical health. Sunlight can help regulate sleep patterns, boost immune function, and enhance mood.

Integrating natural materials like wood and stone can create a more natural and organic feel to a room, bringing nature to the indoors.

Another biophilic design element is water, which also has a positive impact on human well-being. Incorporating water features like small fountains or images of water promotes feelings of relaxation and tranquility, creating a soothing atmosphere.

Even the use of colors has a biophilic effect on spaces. Using earthy tones like greens, blues, and browns creates a calming, natural feeling. Animal prints, shells, spirals, oval and tubular shapes, and natural materials simulate natural features. Most of these elements are easy to add.

The biophilic design also has a significant impact on shaping the way people live in urban environments. With a large proportion of the population living in densely populated urban areas, incorporating biophilic design elements has become critical in creating spaces that are conducive to well-being and productivity. Biophilic design can help to improve air quality, reduce stress and anxiety, promote creativity, and boost overall health and happiness.

Incorporating biophilic design elements can have many benefits in creating beautiful, functional, and healthy indoor spaces that promote well-being. Find a link to more information about the biophilic design in the reference section.

# Color

I could not complete my book about art in home staging without a chapter about color. The relationship between color and art can be both serious and playful at the same time. Colors can be tricky—they can make or break a room. It's like choosing what to wear on a date—you want to look fabulous, but not flashy.

As I mentioned at the beginning of this book, it's written on the assumption that you've done all the work on your house necessary for it to be ready for showcasing as the last step in home staging. And I hope you painted the walls a light neutral color in case they weren't. If you haven't, please do so now.

## Best Colors for the Walls

Neutral wall colors are best for selling homes. What these colors do for the house is they make walls not very noticeable. The walls are just a background. You don't want buyers to remember the color of the walls. If they do, it may be for the right or wrong reason, and you don't want to gamble with that. If the buyers don't like the color of the walls, they may consequently not like the property. You may wonder why. Don't they know it's so easy to repaint? Yup, they do. But many of them don't want to repaint now. They have a lot on their plate already; the move is stressful. They just want to move in and then remodel, repaint, renovate, and redesign… someday. Make it easy for them to love your home and to make an offer. Paint your walls, preferably in one color throughout. This will create an effortless flow. It's one of the most effective and inexpensive ways to refresh and uplift your home and make it move-in ready.

The neutral wall colors I recommend for home staging are white, off-white, light gray, light beige, greige, and linen.

White is often the go-to color for neutral walls and for a good reason. It is fresh and timeless. It also creates a sense of space and openness, which can be appealing to buyers looking for a larger home. However, too much white can also make a room feel cold and uninviting, so it's important to balance it with other colors by using colorful art and accessories.

Off-white is another popular choice and is a great option if you want to add a bit of warmth to your walls. Shades such as cream and ivory can all create a cozy, inviting feel while still maintaining a neutral aesthetic.

Light gray is another versatile option that can work well with a variety of decor styles. You can pair it with both warm and cool tones, and can even create a subtle backdrop for more dramatic accents or artwork.

Light beige and greige (a combination of gray and beige) are also popular choices for neutral walls. These colors can add warmth and depth to a space and are great for creating a cohesive, calming atmosphere.

Linen is a newer trend in neutral wall colors and is popular in modern farmhouse and Scandinavian design styles. It has a warm, natural feel and pairs well with other earthy tones and organic textures.

## Other Uses of Color

Now let's talk about colors other than on the walls. There is a school of thought in the home staging industry that everything should be neutral. The intensity and the hue may vary but still stay in the neutral color category. Well, this is not what I think. Color plays a very important role in how people perceive space because of physiological and psychological responses to it, and I don't want to leave things to chance. That's why I love using a lot of color in artwork and accessories. Also, because I just love colors.

Two neutrals that can be very effective in staging are black and white. This palette brings a high-contrast graphic look, and it works best in modern interiors. Adding one more color to the black-and-white color scheme will make the additional color pop more powerful. Keep that in mind.

Color is such a limitless topic, I won't even try to cover a fraction. All I want to tell you is that it can help you elevate the presentation of your home immensely.

Start with the mood you want to create. Look at the colors that help create this mood (there is also a link in the reference section) and then choose items featuring these colors. Start with wall art, then move to textiles, and then to accessories.

In a bedroom, you may want a restful, tranquil space. Soothing shades of blue, green, and neutral work well in a bedroom. These colors are calming and promote relaxation, making them ideal for a space where anyone entering the room will want to unwind and get some much-needed rest.

A family room should have a cozy and warm feeling. Earthy tones such as warm browns, deep greens, and rich yellows create a space that is inviting and comfortable. These warm colors are perfect for a room where the buyers will want to spend quality time with family and friends.

For the living room, a more upscale and sophisticated feeling may be more appropriate. Classic colors such as grays, whites, and beiges, as well as bold colors like reds, work well in the living room. These colors create a timeless and elegant atmosphere that is perfect for entertaining guests.

## Color Rules

There are a few rules I recommend you to follow.

One is called "stay in the lane". That means choosing either all warm or all cool colors and not combining them. Remember, yellow and red can be cool, and blue and purple can be warm. Even though your intuition may tell you otherwise. All pure colors (saturates) and tints (added white) are cool, and all shades (added black) and tones (added gray) are warm. By choosing either warm or cool colors for a room, you can create a cohesive, inviting space that feels harmonious and well-balanced.

Another rule is called "cross-pollinating" when there is a certain proportion between the colors used in the room. To strike the right balance, aim for 60% walls, 30% furniture, and 10% accents. The other rooms can reverse the proportion. Using too much of one color can be overwhelming and can throw off the balance of the room while using too many colors can create a chaotic, cluttered feel.

Besides selecting warm or cool hues and balancing color proportions, it's also important to ensure that at least one color from your overall color palette is present in every room in some capacity. This can help tie different areas of your home together and create a cohesive design. If your overall color palette includes shades of blue and green, for example, you might incorporate blue throw pillows in the living room, green pottery items in the kitchen, and a blue and green wall art piece in the bedroom.

I mentioned earlier that I recommend painting your walls in one color throughout for an effortless flow. It's also easier to create cross-pollination and balance color proportions when the walls are the same neutral color in the entire space. When there is a common thread of color flowing throughout all rooms, it creates a better balance and harmony in the entire house.

These rules can be broken to create balanced and beautiful spaces, however, it takes some practice.

When staging your home, color is a powerful tool that can help create a warm, inviting, and cohesive space. By following these rules for choosing colors, you can ensure that each room feels harmonious and well-designed and will make your potential buyers fall in love with your home and buy it.

## Conclusion

Well, this is what I wanted to tell you in this short book about staging your home for a successful sale using art in its various forms. I hope if you apply these ideas you'll achieve your goal: the buyers will fall in love with your home and it will be sold fast and for top dollar. Many of these principles you can also use in your new home, only then, you can be even more creative because this time you'll be designing it for you and your family. You can break the rules as long as you like the "finished product". I'm sure you'll have lots of fun and will want to learn more. Maybe like me, one day you'll want to become a home stager too and help other homeowners with their properties.

Thank you for choosing my book and taking the time to read it! I am thrilled to share with you unique insights on creating a beautiful and welcoming space for buyers. I really hope that you enjoyed it and you'll have lots of fun staging your home with art.

## CONCLUSION

If you found it helpful, I kindly ask you to consider leaving a review on Amazon or on the platform you bought it from. Your honest thoughts and experiences can help other homeowners who are considering purchasing my book.

Thank you again for your support, and I can't wait to hear what you think!

If you want to get in touch with me, you can contact me directly. My email is valerie@atfirstsightstaging.ca

I'll be happy to answer any home staging or decorating questions you may have. You can also visit my website www.atfirstsightstaging.ca and sign up for my monthly newsletter.

**Happy staging and decorating!**

# References

Home Stratosphere. (2018, July 20). *52 Different Types of Wall Art Explained*. Https://Www.Homestratosphere.Com/. Retrieved July 12, 2022, from https://www.homestratosphere.com/types-of-wall-art

Better Homes & Gardens. (2022, May 24). *18 Effortless Ways to Style Bookshelf Decor*. Https://Www.Bhg.Com/. Retrieved July 12, 2022, from https://www.bhg.com/decorating/storage/shelves/get-picture-perfect-bookshelves

Artiplanto. (n.d.). *ALL POTTED ARTIFICIAL PLANT*. Https://Www.Artiplanto.Com/. Retrieved July 12, 2022, from https://www.artiplanto.com/collections/artificial-plants-canada-us-onl

Architectural Digest. (2017, June 16). *8 Formulas for Perfectly Mismatched Throw Pillow*. Https://Www.Architecturaldigest.Com/. Retrieved July 12, 2022, from

REFERENCES

https://www.architecturaldigest.com/story/throw-pillows-formula

Crate & Barrel. (n.d.-d).
*How to Style Throw Pillow*. Https://Www.Crateandbarrel.Com. Retrieved July 12, 2022, from
https://www.crateandbarrel.ca/decorating-and-accessories/throw-pillow-ideas

All Posters. (n.d.).
*Wall Art*. Https://Www.Allposters.Com/. Retrieved July 12, 2022, from
https://www.allposters.com

Art.com. (n.d.).
*Wall Art*. Https://Www.Art.Com/. Retrieved July 12, 2022, from
https://www.art.com

Pebble Magazine. (2022, March 30).
*Biophilic Design: What Is It And How Do You Make It Work For Your Home* Https://Pebblemag.Com/Magazine/Living/Biophilic-Design. Retrieved July 12, 2022, from
https://pebblemag.com/magazine/living/biophilic-design

The Art Career Project. (2019, June 18).
*Introduction to the Psychology of Color For Interior Designers*. Https://Theartcareerproject.Com/. Retrieved July 13, 2022, from

https://theartcareerproject.com/psychology-of-color-interior-design

# About the Author

Valerie Westra is a Canadian Certified Staging Professional (CCSP®) and the owner of At First Sight Home Staging Solutions. Since 2009 she has staged hundreds of homes. She lives in Victoria, British Columbia.

**You can connect with me on:**
🌐 https://atfirstsightstaging.ca

www.ingramcontent.com/pod-product-compliance
Lightning Source LLC
Chambersburg PA
CBHW071254070526

44583CB00017B/2471